Exploring America
Quiz and Exam Book

Exploring America Quiz and Exam Book (2019 Edition)
ISBN: 978-1-60999-121-0

Cover Image: Young women studying on the campus of the Saxon Mills school, Spartanburg, South Carolina, 1918, Goldsberry Collection / Library of Congress

Printed in the United States of America

Notgrass Company
975 Roaring River Rd.
Gainesboro, TN 38562
1-800-211-8793
notgrass.com

Quiz on Unit 1

Review the Student Review questions on Lessons 1-5.

True or False

______ 1. History helps us understand the present.

______ 2. Nations generally believe that their own ways and perspectives are correct and superior to those of other cultures.

______ 3. Most events and people can be clearly characterized as good or bad.

______ 4. God is working out His plan for human history until time on earth ends.

______ 5. A major factor influencing the events of history is the desire to control one's destiny and often the destiny of others.

______ 6. George Santayana wrote that those who cannot remember the past are condemned to repeat it.

______ 7. The Renaissance resulted in a narrowing of horizons for human thought and activity.

______ 8. The Crusades introduced the geography, cultures, and riches of the East to Europeans.

______ 9. The chief motivation felt by Europeans for traveling to Asia was to convert the Chinese.

______ 10. We are confident that Native Americans came to the western hemisphere by means of a land bridge across the Bering Strait.

______ 11. The ruler of Portugal sponsored Columbus' first voyage.

______ 12. Magellan's crew sailed around the world.

______ 13. England was the dominant European power in North America until about 1600.

______ 14. Hernando Cortes led the conquest of the Aztecs.

______ 15. Worldview means the ability to draw a map accurately.

Short Answer

16. What does the word Renaissance mean? ______________________________

17. What European explorer is thought to have landed on the eastern coast of North America before Columbus? ______________________________

18. What miscalculation did Columbus make regarding the size of the earth?

____

19. What did Spanish explorers want to do with the gold and other riches they found in the New World? ____________________

20. What was the first permanent European settlement in what would become the United States?

____

Quiz on Unit 2

Review the Student Review questions on Lessons 6-10.

______ 1. One of the greatest abuses in Roman Catholicism was the selling of:
(a) property (c) relics
(b) church positions (d) indulgences

______ 2. Martin Luther protested Catholic practices by posting his:
(a) 95 Theses (c) Petition to the Pope
(b) Declaration of Conscience (d) Document of Protest

______ 3. The English ruler who broke with Rome and established the Church of England was:
(a) George III
(b) Henry VIII
(c) Elizabeth I
(d) Charles II

______ 4. Newfoundland was claimed for England by:
(a) Christopher Columbus (c) John Cabot
(b) James I (d) Elizabeth I

______ 5. Mary and Elizabeth I were what relation to Henry VIII?
(a) grandmother and mother (c) mother and aunt
(b) sisters (d) daughters

______ 6. The first English attempt to establish a colony in North America was:
(a) Newfoundland (c) Roanoke
(b) Plymouth (d) St. Augustine

______ 7. England's power increased by their defeating in a sea battle in 1588:
(a) the Puritans (c) the Spanish Armada
(b) the Prussian army (d) the Dutch fleet

______ 8. Who became king of England when Elizabeth I died?
(a) Henry VIII (c) Richard II
(b) George III (d) James I

______ 9. The political and economic philosophy that encouraged colonial settlement was:
(a) mercantilism (c) toleration
(b) ipsedixitism (d) democracy

______ 10. Jamestown was all of the following EXCEPT:
(a) the first permanent English settlement in North America
(b) founded in 1607
(c) destroyed by the Croatoan Indians
(d) the place where blacks were first sold into servitude in North America

quiz continued on the next page

______ 11. The colony of Plymouth was settled in 1620 by a group we call:

(a) Anabaptists (c) Deserters
(b) Pilgrims (d) Puritans

______ 12. The colony of Massachusetts Bay was settled in 1630 by a group we call:

(a) Pilgrims (c) Puritans
(b) Anabaptists (d) Separatists

______ 13. Roger Williams founded the colony of:

(a) Connecticut (c) Williams Bay
(b) Rhode Island (d) Pennsylvania

______ 14. What colony was intended to be a haven for English Catholics?

(a) New Jersey (c) Connecticut
(b) New York (d) Maryland

______ 15. What religious group is associated with the founding of Pennsylvania?

(a) Quakers (c) Antiquarians
(b) Anabaptists (d) Latitudinarians

______ 16. In the colonies women:

(a) had few legal rights (c) often were chosen as governors and judges
(b) had more rights than they do today (d) resented their subservience to men

______ 17. The most common occupation of the colonists was:

(a) farming
(b) missionary
(c) banking
(d) silversmith

______ 18. The Half-Way Covenant:

(a) encouraged half-hearted Christianity
(b) allowed a person to give only half of his expected tithe
(c) allowed children of non-church members to get some benefits of church membership
(d) called for settlers and Indians to meet half-way to resolve their differences

______ 19. The two sides in the English Civil War that began in 1642 were the Royalists and the:

(a) Cavaliers
(b) Roundheads
(c) Separatists
(d) Catholics

______ 20. One significance of William and Mary coming to the throne of England was that:

(a) it was the first time a woman had been on the throne
(b) they took the throne at the request and permission of Parliament
(c) it enabled Catholics to have a greater voice in English politics
(d) they wanted to give the American colonies their independence

Quiz on Unit 3

Review the Student Review questions on Lessons 11-15.

_____ 1. Enlightenment thinking:
(a) emphasized natural law and de-emphasized God's role in the world
(b) denied the existence of God altogether
(c) promoted evolution
(d) increased respect for the monarchy

_____ 2. John Locke:
(a) believed in the divine right of kings
(b) applied reason and natural law to human society
(c) opposed Galileo's theories
(d) opposed Isaac Newton's theories

_____ 3. At first, who had ultimate political authority in the English colonies?
(a) the voters
(b) the elected assemblies
(c) the Supreme Court
(d) the king and appointed governors

_____ 4. Who voted for representatives in the colonial assemblies?
(a) all colonists 21 years old or older
(b) all males
(c) free male property owners
(d) free men and male slaves

_____ 5. What colonial militia officer tried to push the French from Fort Duquesne?
(a) John Hancock
(b) George Washington
(c) William Pitt
(d) Benjamin Franklin

_____ 6. One result of the French and Indian War was that:
(a) France helped the colonies during the American Revolution
(b) France took over all of Canada
(c) England was ready to be rid of her American colonies
(d) England ceased building a world empire

_____ 7. The confrontation between Boston citizens and British soldiers on March 5, 1770, is called the:
(a) Boston Tea Party
(b) Act of Defense
(c) Boston Massacre
(d) shot heard 'round the world

_____ 8. What did the first Continental Congress meet to oppose?
(a) royal authority
(b) the Coercive Acts
(c) the Battle of Lexington
(d) the Sons of Liberty

_____ 9. Some churches opposed the Great Awakening revival because:
(a) evangelists charged that there were many dead churches and unconverted clergy
(b) church membership actually decreased as a result of it
(c) a strong movement developed in opposition to a paid clergy
(d) many church members were persuaded to leave the colonies and move to Europe

_____ 10. What American was recognized as the leading preacher of the Great Awakening?
(a) John Harvard
(b) Isaiah Wilkinson
(c) Jedidah Rutgers
(d) Jonathan Edwards

Quiz on Unit 4

Review the Student Review questions on Lessons 16-19.

_____ 1. Who gave the speech that ended, "Give me liberty or give me death"?
(a) George Washington
(b) Patrick Henry
(c) John Adams
(d) Thomas Paine

_____ 2. The outcome of the Battle of Bunker (or Breed's) Hill was:
(a) a costly American victory
(b) a costly British victory
(c) a draw
(d) the loss of New England to the British

_____ 3. Whom did the second Continental Congress appoint as Commander of the Continental Army?
(a) John Hancock
(b) John Dickinson
(c) George Washington
(d) Paul Revere

_____ 4. The author of "Common Sense" and "The Crisis" was:
(a) Thomas Jefferson
(b) Thomas Paine
(c) John Dickinson
(d) George Washington

_____ 5. The main author of the Declaration of Independence was:
(a) Thomas Paine
(b) John Adams
(c) Benjamin Franklin
(d) Thomas Jefferson

_____ 6. The grievances stated in the Declaration of Independence were directed against:
(a) the rich merchants of Britain
(b) the king
(c) Parliament
(d) the royal governors in the colonies

_____ 7. The year of 1776 was:
(a) the year that the Continental Army reclaimed New York City
(b) the year that the colonies declared their independence from Great Britain
(c) the decisive year for the outcome of the Revolutionary War
(d) a year with no major U.S. losses

_____ 8. Washington led his troops to a surprise victory on Christmas night 1776 at:
(a) Trenton (b) Princeton (c) Hoboken (d) Perth Amboy

_____ 9. The turning point of the war was:
(a) the Battle of Saratoga
(b) the surrender of New York City
(c) the Battle of Valley Forge
(d) the Battle of Kaskasia

_____ 10. The turning point of the war in the South was:
(a) the Battle of King's Mountain
(b) the Battle of Camden
(c) the Battle of Shiloh
(d) the Battle of Cowpens

_____ 11. What British general surrendered his army to Washington at Yorktown, Virginia?
(a) Burgoyne
(b) Arnold
(c) Cornwallis
(d) Cromwell

quiz continued on the next page

_____ 12. How was the American Revolution a civil war?
(a) The North fought against the South. (c) It divided communities and families.
(b) Cavaliers fought against Roundheads. (d) Republicans battled Democrats

_____ 13. One major failure that led to the British defeat in the American Revolution was:
(a) the failure of British diplomacy in handling the British relationship with the colonies
(b) the failure of British spies to infiltrate the American army and government
(c) the failure of the Anglican churches to support the royal government
(d) the failure of Canada to support the British

_____ 14. America's victory in the Revolutionary War:
(a) caused more Indian attacks in the trans-Appalachian region
(b) resulted in the United States losing control of the area between the states and the Mississippi River
(c) encouraged settlement of western lands
(d) prohibited settlement of western lands

_____ 15. As a result of the Revolutionary War:
(a) American society went through a tremendous upheaval
(b) American government came close to becoming a monarchy
(c) the southern colonies seceded from the northern colonies
(d) the American economy suffered greatly

_____ 16. What did many state constitutions that were written in the 1780s provide?
(a) the right of every person to vote
(b) universal health care
(c) a requirement to teach French in public schools
(d) a bill of rights

_____ 17. What economic opportunity did America offer that Great Britain did not?
(a) land ownership and building wealth (c) better life insurance options
(b) joining a labor union (d) the right to invest in the stock market

_____ 18. What was the first governing document of the United States?
(a) the Constitution (c) the Declaration of Independence
(b) the Articles of Confederation (d) the Proclamation of 1763

_____ 19. Daniel Boone:
(a) led settlers through the Cumberland Gap
(b) led the Americans at the Battle of King's Mountain
(c) was royal governor of Kentucky
(d) was a myth

_____ 20. What was a major issue that delayed the ratification of the Articles of Confederation by all of the states?
(a) what to call the chief executive
(b) whether to admit New York
(c) establishing diplomatic relations with Great Britain
(d) the handling of western lands

Quiz on Unit 5

Review the Student Review questions on Lessons 21-24.

Matching, Part 1

_____ 1. George Washington was the chairman.	A. *The Federalist*
_____ 2. It set the pattern for how territories would become states.	B. Constitutional Convention
_____ 3. It dealt with how slaves would be counted for representation and taxation.	C. Electors
_____ 4. It dealt with how the states would be represented in Congress.	D. A Federal income tax
_____ 5. They really choose the President.	E. Antifederalists
_____ 6. Essays published to encourage ratification of the Constitution	F. Great Compromise
_____ 7. The term used to describe those who opposed ratification of the Constitution	G. Northwest Ordinance
_____ 8. The 16th Amendment enables this	H. Presidential succession
_____ 9. The most prominent and active delegate at the Constitutional Convention	I. Three-Fifths Compromise
_____ 10. The 25th Amendment provides for this	J. James Madison

quiz continued on the next page

Matching, Part 2

_____ 11. What portion of the Senate is elected every two years?	K. Separation of powers
_____ 12. When the President doesn't sign a bill but doesn't send it back to Congress, either	L. The House of Representatives
_____ 13. Something the framers feared	M. The Senate
_____ 14. Its members serve six-year terms.	N. right to keep and bear arms
_____ 15. The length of the President's term	O. commander in chief
_____ 16. Describes how the different branches of government have different responsibilities	P. Pocket veto
_____ 17. Where bills go that are introduced in Congress	Q. Three-fourths
_____ 18. A limitation on government, giving it the ability to do only what it is expressly permitted to do	R. District, Appeals, Supreme
_____ 19. Ways that the branches of government limit the powers of each other	S. Democracy
_____ 20. The president's role regarding the operation of the Federal government	T. four years
_____ 21. Guaranteed by the 2nd Amendment	U. Committee
_____ 22. The entire body is up for election every two years.	V. Oversees the executive branch
_____ 23. The levels of the Federal court system	W. Checks and balances
_____ 24. The fraction of states that must ratify a proposed Constitutional amendment for it to take effect	X. One-third
_____ 25. The President's role with the military	Y. Enumerated powers

History Exam on Units 1-5

Review the quizzes on Units 1-5.

1. George Santayana said that people who cannot remember the past are what?

 ____

2. What introduced the geography, cultures, and riches of the East to Europeans?

 ____

3. What is the name given to the period of intellectual inquiry, exploration, and artistic expression in Europe following the Middle Ages? ______________________________

4. Who led the conquest of the Aztecs in Mexico? ______________________________

5. What European explorer is thought to have landed on the eastern coast of North America before Columbus?

 ____

6. Whose crew sailed around the world? ______________________________

7. What was the first permanent European settlement in what would become the United States?

 ____

8. What English king broke with Rome and established the Church of England? ____________

9. Who sailed to Newfoundland for England in 1497? ______________________________

10. What was the first attempt by the English to establish a colony in North America?

 ____

11. The English navy's defeat of what in 1588 increased English power in the world?

 ____

12. What was the first permanent English settlement in North America, and when was it founded? ______________________________

exam continued on the next page

13. What group founded Plymouth? ______

14. What group founded Massachusetts Bay? ______

15. What colony was begun as a haven for English Catholics? ______

16. Who wrote and posted 95 Theses questioning Catholic practices? ______

17. Who founded the colony of Rhode Island? ______

18. What religious group is associated with the founding of Pennsylvania? ______

19. What was the most common occupation among English colonists? ______

20. What colonial officer tried to push the French out of Fort Duquesne? ______

21. The philosophical movement that emphasized natural law and de-emphasized the role of God in the world is commonly called what? ______

22. Who won the French and Indian War? ______

23. What is the name given to the confrontation between Boston citizens and British soldiers on March 5, 1770? ______

24. Who gave the speech that included, "Give me liberty, or give me death"?

______

25. What British general surrendered to Washington at Yorktown, Virginia? ______

26. Who led thousands of settlers through the Cumberland Gap? ______

27. What was the first governing document of the United States?

______

28. In what year did the Constitutional Convention meet? ______

exam continued on the next page

29. Who was the chairman of the Constitutional Convention?

____

30. What issue did the Three-Fifths Compromise address?

____

____

31. What is the title given to the collection of essays published to encourage ratification of the Constitution? ____

32. Who was the most prominent and active delegate at the Constitutional Convention?

____

33. What is the length of a term for a member of the House of Representatives? ______________

34. What is the length of a Senator's term? ______________________________

35. What is the length of the President's term? ______________________________

36. What is the fraction of states that must ratify a proposed Constitutional amendment for it to take effect? ______________________________

37. What fraction of the Senate is elected every two years? ______________________

38. What is the term that describes the President's role with the military? ______________

____

39. What is the term used to describe the ways that the three branches of government limit each other's powers? ______________________________

40. What right is guaranteed by the 2nd Amendment? ______________________________

On the next History Exam (for Units 6-10), you will be asked to list the presidents of the United States in order from George Washington to James K. Polk. Other future exams will ask for a longer list of presidents.

English Exam on Units 1-5

This exam covers the following documents in American Voices: Bay Psalm Book *(page 6), poems by Anne Bradstreet (page 7),* New England Primer *(pages 8-9), the introduction to* Poor Richard's Almanack *(page 10), poems by Phillis Wheatley (pages 34-35),* Common Sense *(pages 38-42),* The Crisis *(pages 47-48),* The Federalist *(pages 72-76 and page 112 in the text), "Concorn Hymn" (page 137), and "Paul Revere's Ride" (pages 139-142). Also review the box on page 46 of the text as well as* The Scarlet Letter *and the literary analysis of it in the* Student Review, *pages 16-18.*

Part 1—Matching

_____ 1. Anne Bradstreet

_____ 2. Bay Psalm Book

_____ 3. New England Primer

_____ 4. Journals

_____ 5. Benjamin Franklin

_____ 6. Henry Wadsworth Longfellow

_____ 7. Ralph Walso Emerson

_____ 8. Thomas Paine

_____ 9. Phillis Wheatley

_____ 10. The Federalist

A. Poor Richard's Almanack

B. "Common Sense," "The Crisis"

C. Essays published to support ratification of the Constitution

D. "To My Dear and Loving Husband"

E. "Concord Hymn"

F. Slave who wrote poetry

G. "Paul Revere's Ride"

H. First writing by Europeans in America

I. First book printed in America

J. Schoolbook used for many years in America

Part 2—Questions on The Scarlet Letter

1. What did the scarlet letter that Hester Prynne wore stand for? ______________________________

2. How were people mistaken about Arthur Dimmesdale's character?

exam continued on the next page

____

3. How does *The Scarlet Letter* show the effect of sin that is hidden and sin that is brought into the open? ____

____

Part 3—Identify the source of these quotations, using these choices. Write your answers in the blanks beside the quotations.

Poor Richard's Almanack
The Federalist Number 10
The Scarlet Letter
"The Crisis"

1. "By a faction, I understand a number of citizens, whether amounting to a majority or a minority of the whole, who are united and actuated by some common impulse of passion, or of interest, adverse to the rights of other citizens, or to the permanent and aggregate interests of the community. There are two methods of curing the mischiefs of faction: the one, by removing its causes; the other, by controlling its effects." __________________________

2. "These are the times that try men's souls. The summer soldier and the sunshine patriot will, in this crisis, shrink from the service of their country; but he that stands it now, deserves the love and thanks of man and woman." ______________________________________

3. "Be slow in chusing a Friend, slower in changing." _________________________________

4. "The same platform or scaffold, black and weather-stained with the storm or sunshine of seven long years, and footworn, too, with the treat of many culprits who had since ascended it, remained standing beneath the balcony of the meeting-house. The minister went up the steps." ____

Bible Exam on Units 1-5

Review the Student Review questions on Lessons 1, 5, 6, 8, 10, 11-13, 20, 25.

1. What was one purpose of the annual festivals that God commanded Israel to observe?

 ____

2. What is meant by the term worldview? ______________________________

 ____

3. What are two elements of a God-centered worldview? ______________________________

 ____

 ____

4. A questionable practice of the medieval Catholic church was the selling of what?

 ____

5. What German priest and scholar challenged this practice? ______________________________

6. What is the term given to the points of debate this priest posted in Wittenberg?

 ____

7. In what year did he post these points of debate? ______________________________

8. What did the Half-Way Covenant do? ______________________________

 ____

9. In 1688 the English Parliament asked what Protestant couple to rule England? ____________

 ____

10. What dissenter founded the colony of Rhode Island? ______________________________

11. What religious group is associated with the founding of Pennsylvania? ______________

 ____

12. How did the Enlightenment change the common view of God and religion?

 ____

 ____

exam continued on the next page

13. What was the Great Awakening? ______________________________

____

____

14. Over what issue did some denominations divide regarding the Great Awakening? ________

____

15. Who was the leading American minister during the Great Awakening?

____

16. Who were two English ministers who helped bring about a spiritual revival in England?

____

____

17. Why was the Great Awakening opposed by some churches?

____

____

18. What kind of institutions were begun in America for the training of ministers?

____

19. Who causes the rise and fall of nations? ______________________________

20. What is the supreme law for Christians? ______________________________

21. What are the two most basic steps of interpretation?

____

____

22. What is the best interpreter of a passage of Scripture? ______________________________

____

23. What was God's most important act? ______________________________

24. What is meant by prooftexting? ______________________________

____

____

25. How should the Bible be read and understood? ______________________________

____

Quiz on Unit 6

Review the Student Review questions on Lessons 26-29.

Matching

_____ 1. Federalist-passed laws intended to limit foreign influence and weaken Republican strength.

_____ 2. Made with Great Britain but widely unpopular

_____ 3. Federalist attempt to control the Federal judiciary

_____ 4. John Adams' nominee for Chief Justice

_____ 5. When George Washington first took the presidential oath

_____ 6. The heads of the executive departments

_____ 7. He believed in rule by the elite and in a strong central government

_____ 8. He served as Vice President under John Adams

_____ 9. Passed in opposition to the Alien and Sedition Acts

_____ 10. Movement opposing Federal taxes

_____ 11. Washington's position for the U.S. with regard to European wars

_____ 12. An attempt by the French to obtain a bribe from American diplomats

_____ 13. Settled issues with Spain

_____ 14. The first President to live in the White House

_____ 15. Part of Hamilton's plan for the country

A. Cabinet

B. National bank

C. Whiskey Rebellion

D. Thomas Jefferson

E. John Marshall

F. 1789

G. Pinckney Treaty

H. Jay Treaty

I. John Adams

J. Neutrality

K. XYZ Affair

L. Virginia and Kentucky Resolutions

M. Alexander Hamilton

N. Alien and Sedition Acts

O. Judiciary Act of 1801

Quiz on Unit 7

Review the Student Review questions on Lessons 31-34.

1. The body that determined the outcome of the election of 1800: ____________________

   ____

2. What Jefferson called his election in 1800: ____________________

3. Leaders of the Corps of Discovery:

   ____________________ ____________________

4. Indian translator for the Corps of Discovery: ____________________

5. The home state of the three Presidents who served from 1801 to 1825: ____________

6. Outlawed during Jefferson's term in office: ____________________

7. Influential Chief Justice of the U.S. Supreme Court: ____________________

8. The city invaded and burned by the British during the War of 1812: ____________

   ____

9. Last battle of the War of 1812: ____________________

10. Canal that connected Buffalo and New York City: ____________________

Quiz on Unit 8

Review the Student Review questions on Lessons 36-39.

True or False

_____ 1. Slave states opposed extending slavery into the territories because they feared it would weaken the slave economy.

_____ 2. Only the southern states had ever allowed slavery.

_____ 3. The Missouri Compromise was engineered by Thomas Jefferson.

_____ 4. As a result of the Missouri Compromise, all of the area in the Louisiana Territory north of Missouri was open to slavery.

_____ 5. The Monroe Doctrine warned European nations that the U.S. might get involved in their domestic issues.

_____ 6. The Monroe Doctrine dealt with U.S. policy toward Native Americans.

_____ 7. In the 1824 election, John Quincy Adams received the most popular votes.

_____ 8. In the 1820s, the office of vice president was seen as the stepping stone to the presidency.

_____ 9. Andrew Jackson became a national hero as a result of the Battle of Fort McHenry.

_____ 10. After he was President, John Quincy Adams served in the U.S. Senate.

_____ 11. Rachel and Andrew Jackson got married while Andrew was still married to someone else.

_____ 12. Henry Clay and Andrew Jackson were political allies who worked closely together.

_____ 13. Adams defeated Jackson in his bid for re-election in 1828.

_____ 14. Rachel Jackson died after Andrew Jackson was sworn in as President.

_____ 15. Andrew Jackson had never held elected office before he was elected President.

Quiz on Unit 9

Review the Student Review questions on Lessons 41-44,
but not the questions on American literature and American poetry.

Matching

_____ 1. Served as President for one month	A. Henry Clay
_____ 2. Ran from Independence, Missouri, to what is now the American northwest	B. Stephen F. Austin
_____ 3. Believed that states could nullify Federal laws	C. James K. Polk
_____ 4. Democratic presidential candidate in 1844	D. Sam Houston
_____ 5. Whig presidential candidate in 1844	E. Moses Austin
_____ 6. Received a land grant from the Mexican government	F. Oregon Trail
_____ 7. Encouraged people to settle in Texas	G. William Henry Harrison
_____ 8. Old Kinderhook	H. John C. Calhoun
_____ 9. President of the Republic of Texas	I. John Tyler
_____ 10. President who was cast out of the Whig Party	J. Martin Van Buren

Quiz on Unit 10

Review the Student Review questions on Lessons 46-49.

_____ 1. In the ancient world, slaves were often:
(a) blacks
(b) Irish
(c) captives in war
(d) wealthy

_____ 2. The legal standing of slaves in the U.S. was that of:
(a) citizens
(b) diplomats
(c) refugees
(d) property

_____ 3. Nat Turner's rebellion was:
(a) a revolt against slaves being taxed
(b) an uprising of slaves against whites
(c) crushed by the U.S. Army
(d) a reaction by slaves to being exported to Africa

_____ 4. In *The Liberator* William Lloyd Garrison urged:
(a) gradual emancipation
(b) an end to the tax on slaves
(c) a national referendum on slavery
(d) immediate emancipation

_____ 5. Manufacturing helped agriculture by:
(a) removing the excess rural population
(b) taxes that were paid to farmers
(c) inventing new kinds of seeds
(d) the production of labor-saving equipment

_____ 6. Many Irish came to the United States:
(a) because of the potato famine in Ireland
(b) to work on farms in the Midwest
(c) because the British government revoked their citizenship
(d) to play basketball for the Boston Celtics

_____ 7. The goal of the American Colonization Society for slaves was to:
(a) create a colony for them in Texas
(b) create a colony for them in Alabama
(c) resettle them in Africa
(d) resettle them in India

_____ 8. The American Party was sometimes called:
(a) the Know-Nothing Party
(b) the Republican Party
(c) the Democratic Party
(d) the Texas First Party

_____ 9. The development of railroads was helped by:
(a) government assistance to railroad companies
(b) the discovery of iron
(c) slave labor
(d) a tax on horses

_____ 10. Most immigrants did not move to the South because:
(a) they could not understand the southern accent
(b) they would have to compete with slave labor
(c) they did not know how to get there
(d) they were allergic to cotton

History Exam on Units 6-10

Review the quizzes on Units 6-10. You will be asked to list the first eleven presidents in order.

Matching, Part 1

_____ 1. Appointed by John Adams, he was an influential Chief Justice of the Supreme Court. He confirmed the Court's power of judicial review.	A. Meriweather Lewis
_____ 2. A war hero, he was elected as the Whig candidate for President in 1840 but only served one month before his death.	B. Thomas Jefferson
_____ 3. Originally from Tennessee, he worked for the independence of Texas from Mexico and became president of the Republic of Texas.	C. Andrew Jackson
_____ 4. He was a War Hawk who advocated going to war with Great Britain in 1812. He was Secretary of State under John Quincy Adams and ran for President as a Whig against James K. Polk in 1844.	D. Sam Houston
_____ 5. The leader of American forces in the Battle of New Orleans, he felt cheated out of the presidency in 1824. He was elected in 1828 and 1832. His nickname was "Old Hickory."	E. Henry Clay
_____ 6. He was author of the Declaration of Independence, Secretary of State under George Washington, and elected President in what he called the "Revolution of 1800."	F. Stephen F. Austin
_____ 7. He encouraged Americans to move to Texas and settle on the large land grant that his father had received from the Mexican government.	G. William Lloyd Garrison
_____ 8. As editor of The Liberator, he advocated the immediate abolition of slavery.	H. Alexander Hamilton
_____ 9. Secretary of the Treasury under George Washington, he had a different view of government from that of Thomas Jefferson.	I. John Marshall
_____ 10. Led the Corps of Discovery along with William Clark.	J. William Henry Harrison

exam continued on the next page

Matching, Part 2

_____ 11. He was Vice President under Andrew Jackson. His nickname was "Old Kinderhook."	A. James K. Polk
_____ 12. He was a slave who led a rebellion against whites.	B. John C. Calhoun
_____ 13. The son of a President, he was Secretary of State under James Monroe, later President himself, and then served in the U.S. House of Representatives.	C. Martin Van Buren
_____ 14. She was a Native American who served as a translator for the Corps of Discovery.	D. John Adams
_____ 15. A former Democrat from Virginia, he became President upon the death of William Henry Harrison. The Whig Party later cast him out.	E. Nat Turner
_____ 16. He was the Democratic candidate for President in 1844 and was President during the Mexican War.	F. Sacajawea
_____ 17. A southerner who defended slavery and believed that states had the righ to nullify or refuse to enforce Federal laws	G. John Quincy Adams
_____ 18. He was Vice President under George Washington and became the first President to live in the White House.	H. John Tyler

Matching, Part 3

_____ 19. This engineering wonder connected Buffalo with New York City.	W. Monroe Doctrine
_____ 20. Settlers used this path, which ran from Independence, Missouri, to what became the American northwest.	X. Whiskey Rebellion
_____ 21. This American foreign policy statement warned European nations not to become involved in the Western Hemisphere.	Y. Oregon Trail
_____ 22. This was a protest movement against the imposition of a Federal tax.	Z. Erie Canal

exam continued on the next page

23-33. *List the first eleven presidents in order. We've given their first names to get you started.*

1. George ______________________________

2. John ______________________________

3. Thomas ______________________________

4. James ______________________________

5. James ______________________________

6. John ______________________________

7. Andrew ______________________________

8. Martin ______________________________

9. William ______________________________

10. John ______________________________

11. James K. ______________________________

English Exam on Units 6-10

This exam covers shorter works that you have read in these units, one book, the section on "The Growth of American Literature" on pages 228-230 in the text, and the section on "American Poetry" on pages 236-237 in the text.

Identify the author of each work (select from these answers).

Herman Melville	James Fenimore Cooper	David Crockett
Frances E. W. Harper	Oliver Wendell Holms	Francis Scott Key
Emily Dickinson	Walt Whitman	Henry Wadsworth Longfellow
Nathaniel Hawthorne	Francis Parkman	Henry David Thoreau

1. *"The Star-Spangled Banner"* ______________________________
2. *"I Hear America Singing"* ______________________________
3. *"I'm nobody! Who are you?"* ______________________________
4. *"The Arrow and the Song"* ______________________________
5. *"Old Ironsides"* ______________________________
6. *"Civil Disobedience"* ______________________________
7. *"The Great Stone Face"* ______________________________
8. *"Bury Me in a Free Land"* ______________________________
9. *A narrative of his life* ______________________________
10. *Moby Dick* ______________________________
11. *The Last of the Mohicans* ______________________________
12. *The Oregon Trail* ______________________________

13. What is a verse or unit of thought in a poem called? ______________________________

14. What is the term for the accent pattern of rhythm in a poem? ______________________________

15. What is the repetition of initial sounds in successive words? ______________________________

Bible Exam on Units 6-10

Review the Student Review questions on Lessons 30, 35, 40, 45, and 50.

1. Define civil religion. ____________________

____

____

____

2. What Chief Justice was later President of the American Bible Society? ____________________

3. Where did a large camp meeting take place near Lexington, Kentucky? ____________________

4. What is the name given to the religious revival of the early 1800s? ____________________

5. What did many people involved in this revival want to do about denominational organizations? ____________________

6. What term did transcendentalists use for the Deity that they said is in all people and things?

____

7. Who was the leading Christian evangelist in the first half of the 1800s? ____________________

____

8. Who founded Mormonism? ____________________

9. What did William Miller try to predict? ____________________

10. What is the term given to communities begun to establish a perfect way of life?

____

11. How did Jesus protest the activities that were taking place in the temple? ____________________

____

12. With what is God more concerned than material or worldly success? ____________________

Quiz on Unit 11

Review the Student Review questions on Lessons 51-54.

Matching, Part 1

_____ 1. Discovery of gold	A. Battleground for proslavery and antislavery forces
_____ 2. Ostend Manifesto	B. A proposed ban on slavery in territory acquired from Mexico
_____ 3. Popular sovereignty	C. A collection of provisions organized by Henry Clay to avoid disunion
_____ 4. Sectionalism	D. Called for the right to take slaves into all the territories
_____ 5. Gag rule	E. The forbidding in the House of Representatives of petitions regarding the abolition of slavery in the District of Columbia
_____ 6. Nashville Convention	F. The tendency of people in different parts of the country to have different and often conflicting views
_____ 7. Wilmot Proviso	G. An expression of U.S. interest in buying Cuba
_____ 8. Kansas Territory	H. Letting settlers in a territory decide for themselves whether or not to admit slavery
_____ 9. Compromise of 1850	I. 1848 event in California that heightened the debate over slavery in the territories
_____ 10. Fugitive Slave Law	J. Part of the Compromise of 1850 to which many northerners objected

quiz continued on the next page

Matching, Part 2

_____ 11. James Buchanan	K. Slave who lost a Supreme Court decision
_____ 12. John Brown	L. Republican presidential candidate in 1856
_____ 13. John C. Calhoun	M. Gifted orator, senator from Massachusetts
_____ 14. Henry Clay	N. Made vicious speech against slave interests
_____ 15. Stephen Douglas	O. The "Great Compromiser," senator from Kentucky
_____ 16. Millard Fillmore	P. Became President after Taylor's death, supported the Compromise of 1850
_____ 17. John C. Fremont	Q. Senator from Illinois, debated Lincoln
_____ 18. Dred Scott	R. Senator from South Carolina, defended slavery
_____ 19. Charles Sumner	S. Democrat elected President in 1856
_____ 20. Daniel Webster	T. Led raid against Harper's Ferry arsenal

Quiz on Unit 12

Review the Student Review questions on Lessons 56-59.

_____ 1. In 1860 the Democrats:
(a) nominated Abraham Lincoln for President
(b) divided and nominated Abraham Lincoln and Stephen Douglas for President
(c) nominated John Bell for President
(d) divided and nominated Stephen Douglas and John Breckenridge for President

_____ 2. In 1860 the Republican Party:
(a) nominated Stephen Douglas for President
(b) nominated Abraham Lincoln for President
(c) nominated John C. Fremont for President
(d) nominated John Bell for President

_____ 3. In the 1860 presidential election:
(a) Abraham Lincoln lost
(b) Abraham Lincoln dropped out of the race and was elected to the U.S. Senate
(c) Abraham Lincoln won
(d) the House of Representatives chose Abraham Lincoln over Stephen Douglas

_____ 4. Following the 1860 presidential election:
(a) South Carolina seceded from the Union
(b) twelve southern states seceded from the Union
(c) Alabama was the first state to secede from the Union
(d) Maryland and Kentucky seceded from the Union

_____ 5. A Confederate government was formed in February 1861 in what city?
(a) Richmond, Virginia
(b) Columbia, South Carolina
(c) Montgomery, Alabama
(d) Nashville, Tennessee

_____ 6. The President of the Confederate States of America was:
(a) Davis Jefferson
(b) Alexander Stephens
(c) Jefferson Davis
(d) Jeb Stuart

_____ 7. A Constitutional amendment passed by Congress but not considered by the states:
(a) guaranteed slavery where it then existed
(b) guaranteed slavery in the territories
(c) abolished slavery
(d) forbade secession

_____ 8. Before he ran for president in 1860, Abraham Lincoln:
(a) had never debated anyone
(b) had never held public office
(c) as far as we know had never voted
(d) had served one term in the U.S. House

_____ 9. In his first inaugural address, Abraham Lincoln said that the decision about war lay with:
(a) all Americans
(b) the people of the South
(c) the opposing armies
(d) the people who had voted against him

quiz continued on the next page

_____ 10. Confederate forces fired on Fort Sumter after Lincoln:
(a) attempted to resupply the fort
(b) ordered Union troops to fire on them
(c) called them names
(d) read them a speech

_____ 11. Lincoln's call for 75,000 volunteers:
(a) caused the Confederacy to dissolve
(b) angered northern Republicans
(c) led more states to secede
(d) led to the immediate emancipation of slaves

_____ 12. The Confederacy was eventually made up of a total of:
(a) seven states
(b) eleven states
(c) 23 states
(d) 34 states

_____ 13. After the Confederacy was formed:
(a) no Union state practiced slavery
(b) two Union states practiced slavery
(c) four Union states practiced slavery
(d) all Union states practiced slavery

_____ 14. When the Civil War began:
(a) the North was in a better position economically
(b) the South was in a strong position economically
(c) the South offered to abolish slavery
(d) the South had more railroad mileage than the North

_____ 15. The Union Anaconda military strategy included all of the following except:
(a) defending Washington, D.C., and attacking Richmond, Virginia
(b) blockading the Confederate coast
(c) dividing the Confederacy by its major rivers
(d) dropping leaflets from balloons onto major southern cities

_____ 16. The Confederates hoped to:
(a) invade the North and seize the major cities
(b) hold the North to a stalemate and obtain a negotiated peace
(c) break the naval blockade and defeat the Union Navy
(d) take control of Mexico and Cuba to increase its power

_____ 17. The two states that had the most battles in the Civil War were:
(a) Virginia and South Carolina
(b) Maryland and Pennsylvania
(c) Kentucky and Tennessee
(d) Virginia and Tennessee

_____ 18. The outcome of the first Battle of Bull Run (or Manassas Junction) was:
(a) Lincoln's resignation
(b) Davis' resignation
(c) a Union victory
(d) a Confederate victory

_____ 19. New Orleans and the southern Mississippi River were captured for the Union by:
(a) David Farragut
(b) Ulysses S. Grant
(c) Jeb Stuart
(d) Stonewall Jackson

_____ 20. Union forces in Tennessee led by Ulysses S. Grant captured Fort Henry and:
(a) Fort Smith
(b) Fort Donelson
(c) Fort McAlister
(d) Fort Payne

Quiz on Unit 13

Review the Student Review questions on Lessons 61-64.

Matching, Part 1

_____ 1. Braxton Bragg	A. Ineffective general, 1864 Democratic presidential candidate
_____ 2. John Wilkes Booth	B. Led Union capture and burning of Atlanta
_____ 3. Andrew Johnson	C. Last Union general-in-chief appointed by Lincoln
_____ 4. Robert E. Lee	D. Assassin of Abraham Lincoln
_____ 5. U.S. Grant	E. Surrendered to Grant at Appomattox Court House
_____ 6. William Sherman	F. Confederate commander at Battle of Stones River
_____ 7. George McClellan	G. Lincoln's running mate in 1864

Matching, Part 2

_____ 8. Franklin and Nashville	H. Location of Ford's Theater, where Lincoln was shot
_____ 9. Shiloh	I. Confederate victories
_____ 10. Gettysburg	J. Grant took this city by a siege that trapped it against a river.
_____ 11. Vicksburg	K. Battle that occurred after Lee invaded the North for the first time
_____ 12. Stones River and Lookout Mountain	L. Battle after a later invasion of the North by Lee; scene of a famous speech by Lincoln dedicating a cemetery
_____ 13. Fredericksburg and Chickamauga	M. Union victories
_____ 14. Antietam (Sharpsburg)	N. Battles in the last Confederate push in the West
_____ 15. Washington, D.C.	O. Costly Union victory near Corinth, Mississippi

Quiz on Unit 14

Review the Student Review questions on Lessons 66-69.

_____ 1. The agency formed by Congress to help former slaves was the:
(a) Land Grant Bureau
(b) Homestead Bureau
(c) Sharecroppers Bureau
(d) Freedmen's Bureau

_____ 2. The Fourteenth Amendment declared Confederate debts to be:
(a) payable at ten cents on the dollar
(b) the responsibility of former slaves
(c) null and void
(d) the responsibility of the U.S. government

_____ 3. Because blacks were largely shut out from white society, blacks responded by:
(a) seizing the land of former plantations
(b) organizing the Ku Klux Klan
(c) refusing to buy from white merchants
(d) organizing black churches and fraternal groups

____ 4. The Military Reconstruction Act put the former states into:
(a) a separate country
(b) five military districts
(c) black states and white states
(d) one large, undivided state

_____ 5. Black codes were:
(a) state laws that restricted the rights of blacks
(b) plans to give blacks educational opportunities
(c) plans to give blacks segregated areas of farm land
(d) attempts to include blacks in the political process

_____ 6. When the Republican-controlled Congress convened in December of 1865:
(a) the House impeached Andrew Johnson
(b) Congress rejected the representatives from the former Confederate states
(c) the Confederate states were readmitted to the Union
(d) the Democrats regained control of Congress

_____ 7. People who farmed and received a portion of the harvest as pay were called:
(a) freedmen
(b) tenants
(c) scalawags
(d) sharecroppers

_____ 8. The Homestead Act:
(a) gave former slaves the property of their former masters
(b) enabled people to receive land free by living on it or farming it for five years
(c) outlawed racial discrimination in home sales
(d) allowed former Confederate soldiers to return to their homes

_____ 9. Congress oversaw Radical Reconstruction by creating the:
(a) Joint Committee on Reconstruction
(b) Freedmen's Bureau
(c) President Pro Tem of the Senate
(d) Homestead Act

quiz continued on the next page

_____ 10. In the 1866 congressional election:
(a) Democrats won a majority of seats in Congress
(b) Radical Republicans increased their majority in Congress
(c) blacks won a majority of seats from the South
(d) carpetbaggers were outlawed

_____ 11. The Fourteenth Amendment:
(a) outlawed secession
(b) gave blacks confiscated property held by the U.S. government
(c) defined citizenship and guaranteed the legal rights of citizens
(d) created a system of representation that gave a certain percentage of seats to blacks

_____ 12. Before Andrew Johnson became Vice President, he had been:
(a) majority leader of the Senate
(b) a large slaveowner
(c) military governor of Tennessee
(d) ambassador to Great Britain

_____ 13. Carpetbaggers were:
(a) contractors who made huge profits on carpeting government buildings
(b) Democrats who acted like Republicans
(c) northerners who moved to the South during Reconstruction
(d) southerners who became Republicans

_____ 14. The Tenure of Office Act said:
(a) no member of Congress could be impeached as long as he held his current office
(b) the president could not fire any appointee who had been confirmed by the Senate
(c) the president served at the discretion of Congress
(d) General Grant had to remain as General of the Army until 1870

_____ 15. In Johnson's impeachment trial:
(a) Johnson avoided being convicted and removed from office by one vote
(b) prosecutors unveiled new evidence of wrongdoing
(c) the President Pro Tem of the Senate resigned
(d) the Democrats walked out and refused to vote

Quiz on Unit 15

Review the Student Review questions on Lessons 71-74.

True or False

1. _____ The Grant Administration was characterized by very few serious scandals.

2. _____ Horace Greeley was the official presidential nominee of the Republican Party in 1872.

3. _____ Democrats regained power in the South in part because whites all across America had a commitment to equality for blacks.

4. _____ The discovery of gold, silver, and copper mines in the West encouraged people to move there.

5. _____ The years after the Civil War saw little conflict with Native Americans.

6. _____ American cities increased in population after the Civil War as a new wave of immigrants came to the country.

7. _____ The transcontinental railroad was built between Omaha, Nebraska, and Los Angeles, California.

8. _____ The 1876 presidential contest was between Rutherford B. Hayes and Samuel J. Tilden.

9. _____ The 1876 presidential election was decided by the U.S. Supreme Court.

10. _____ Democrats accepted Hayes as the winner of the 1876 election in return for his agreeing to remove the remaining Union troops from the South and agreeing to appoint a southerner as postmaster general.

History Exam on Units 11-15

Review the quizzes on Units 11-15. You will be asked to list the first nineteen presidents in order.

1. The discovery of what in California in 1848 led to a heightened debate over slavery in the U.S. territories? ______________________________

2. What was the term used for the idea that settlers in a territory should decide for themselves whether or not to admit slavery? ______________________________

3. To what part of the Compromise of 1850 did many northerners object?

   ____

4. What territory became a battleground for proslavery and antislavery forces?

   ____

5. What state did Henry Clay represent in Congress? ______________________________

6. This South Carolinian was a Senator, Secretary of War, Secretary of tate, and Vice President. He was also a strong defender of slavery. ______________________________

7. This slave lost a Supreme Court case in which he claimed that he should be free.

   ____

8. This Senator from Illinois debated Abraham Lincoln in an 1858 Senate race and ran for President in 1860. ______________________________

9. Who led a raid on a military arsenal at Harper's Ferry, Virginia, in 1859?

   ____

10. There were four candidates in the 1860 presidential contest: Stephen Douglas, John Bell, John Breckenridge, and ______________________________

exam continued on the next page

11. What state was the first to secede following the 1860 election? ____________________

12. Who was president of the Confederacy? ____________________

13. The Confederate government formed in what city and state in February 1861? It later moved to Richmond, Virginia.

____

14. Confederate forces fired on what Federal military facility after President Lincoln tried to resupply it? ____________________

15. The Confederacy was eventually made up of a total of how many states?. ____________

16. After the Confederacy formed, how many states in the Union practiced slavery? ________

17. What general led Union forces to victory at Fort Henry, Fort Donelson, Shiloh, and Vicksburg? ____________________

18. What small town in south central Pennsylvania was the scene of a major battle after Lee invaded the North and was later the scene of a famous speech by Lincoln as he dedicated a cemetery? ____________________

19. Who was Lincoln's running mate in 1864? ____________________

20. An ineffective general, this man was the 1864 Democratic candidate for President.

____

21. The battles at Franklin and at this Tennessee capital city were the last Confederate push in the West. ________________ ____________________

22. What Union general oversaw the capture and burning of Atlanta and the march to the sea across Georgia? ____________________

23. In April of 1865, who surrendered to Grant at Appomattox Court House? ____________

exam continued on the next page

24. Who assassinated Lincoln? ______________________________

25. What agency was formed by the Federal government to help former slaves?

____

26. What is the term given to those who received a portion of the crop for their work on farms?

____

27. State laws that restricted the rights of blacks were called what? ______________

____

28. Which Constitutional amendment, passed after the Civil War, defined citizenship and guaranteed the legal rights of citizens? ______________________________

29. What President faced an impeachment trial that failed to convict him by one vote?

____

30. What President's administration was marked by several major scandals? ______________

____

31. What act of Congress enabled people to receive free land if they lived on it or farmed it for five years? ______________________________

32. What is the two-word term we give to the project that ran between Omaha, Nebraska, and Sacramento, California and was built by two companies, the Central Pacific and Union Pacific? ______________________________

33. The presidential election of 1876 was marked by uncertainties and irregularities. In negotiations between Democratic and Republican leaders to settle the question, the Democrats agreed to support whose election if he promised to remove the remaining Federal troops from the South and to name a southerner as postmaster general?

____

34-52. List the first nineteen presidents in order.

1. George ______________________________
2. John ______________________________
3. Thomas ______________________________
4. James ______________________________
5. James ______________________________
6. John ______________________________
7. Andrew ______________________________
8. Martin ______________________________
9. William ______________________________
10. John ______________________________
11. James K. ______________________________
12. Zachary ______________________________
13. Millard ______________________________
14. Franklin ______________________________
15. James ______________________________
16. Abraham ______________________________
17. Andrew ______________________________
18. Ulysses S. ______________________________
19. Rutherford B. ______________________________

English Exam on Units 11-15

This exam covers these works: Uncle Tom's Cabin, *"The Man Without a Country," "O Captain! My Captain!",* Co. Aytch, *and* Humourous Stories and Sketches. *You should also review the literary analysis of the books in the Student Review.*

1. Write a five-sentence paragraph on why *Uncle Tom's Cabin* had a major impact on the debate over slavery in the decade before the Civil War.

2. Describe in three sentences how Philip Nolan changed his view of the United States during his sentence.

3. With what imagery and emotion does "O Captain! My Captain!" express grief at Lincoln's death?

exam continued on the next page

4. Write a five-sentence paragraph on the significance of *Co. Aytch* as a Civil War memoir.

5. In a five-sentence paragraph, summarize one piece from *Humorous Stories and Sketches* and describe its humor.

Bible Exam on Units 11-15

Review the Student Review questions on Lessons 55, 60, 65, 70, and 75.

1. What are some ways in which people differ from each other? ____________________

2. How can differences be a source of strength? ____________________

3. How might differences be a source of conflict? ____________________

4. What major ethnic and religious difference did Christ bridge? ____________________

5. How should Christians handle differences in gifts and abilities? ____________________

6. How should Christians handle differences of opinion? ____________________

7. How is unity among Christians a powerful message to the world? ____________________

8. Name one Old Testament teaching or incident that indicates that war is acceptable in certain circumstances. ____________________

9. What teachings of Jesus oppose violence? ____________________

exam continued on the next page

10. Why should Christians pray for peace? ______________________________

____

____

11. What is the term for someone who refuses to serve in the military because of his beliefs?

____

12. How can good come from war? ______________________________

____

____

13. What printed religious material was distributed to soldiers during the Civil War?

____

14. What religious activities took place in the soldiers' camps? ______________________________

____

15. What was the religion of the lost cause? ______________________________

____

____

____

16. What had not happened in Jerusalem even many years after former captives had returned?

____

17. Who led the rebuilding project in Jerusalem? ______________________________

18. How did he make it a community effort? ______________________________

____

19. What is a dilemma involved in medical progress? ______________________________

____

____

____

20. How does God define progress?

____

Quiz on Unit 16

Review the Student Review questions on Lessons 76-79.
On this quiz you will be asked to complete a list of the first 24 Presidents in order.

1. What were the names given to the two wings of the Republican Party in 1880?

   ____

2. How did President Hayes end Reconstruction? ______________________________

   ____

   ____

3. Chester Arthur became President in 1881 upon the death of whom, a few weeks after he had been assassinated? ______________________________

4. This assassination led to reform in what area with the passage of the Pendleton Act? ______

   ____

5. Which party gained a majority in the House in the 1890 mid-term election? ______________

   ____

6. Did President Cleveland generally support or oppose bills granting pensions for veterans?

   ____

7. Who was the Republican presidential nominee in 1888? ______________________________

8. What law was an attempt to regulate and control business combinations that were in restraint of trade? ______________________________

   ____

9. What major change was taking place in the U.S. during this period? ______________________

   ____

10. The main purpose of the Interstate Commerce Act was to regulate what industry?

    ____

quiz continued on the next page

11. Bimetallism was the policy of using what two metals as the standard for money?

____

12. What was the third party formed in the early 1890s primarily by farmers who felt that they were being overlooked by the Republicans and Democrats? ______________________

Quiz on Unit 17

Review the Student Review questions on Lessons 81-84.

Matching, Part 1

_____ 1. Finance capitalism	A. Southern Democrats
_____ 2. Corporation	B. Agreements that brought many immigrants to the U.S.
_____ 3. Contract labor	C. The business of managing investments in companies
_____ 4. The Redeemers	D. The first big industry
_____ 5. Ellis Island	E. A chartered business that is a legal person
_____ 6. Railroads	F. Immigrant processing center in New York Harbor

Matching, Part 2

_____ 7. Molly Maguires	G. Became wealthy in shipping and railroads
_____ 8. Terence Powderly	H. Socialist leader of the American Railway Union
_____ 9. James Buchanan Duke	I. Became a wealthy leader in the oil industry
_____ 10. Aaron Montgomery Ward	J. Founded the American Tobacco Company
_____ 11. Eugene V. Debs	K. Involved in the coal mining industry
_____ 12. Cornelius Vanderbilt	L. Leader of the Knights of Labor
_____ 13. John D. Rockefeller	M. Pioneered in catalog sales

Matching, Part 3

_____ 14. New South	N. Convicted after the Haymarket Riot
_____ 15. Wild West show	O. Issues in the West in the late 1800s
_____ 16. Electric power	P. Industrial Workers of the World
_____ 17. Anarchists	Q. Open to industry, less dependent on farming
_____ 18. Wobblies	R. Major events that attracted millions
_____ 19. World's fairs or expositions	S. Popular form of entertainment in the period
_____ 20. Water rights and fencing	T. Contributed to the Second Industrial Revolution

Quiz on Unit 18

Review the Student Review questions on Lessons 86-89.

1. ______________________ Black educator who accepted social segregation and discrimination

2. ______________________ Revenue law passed by Congress but declared unconstitutional by the Supreme Court

3. ______________________ Republican presidential nominee in 1896; gave the "Cross of Gold" speech

4. ______________________ Term used for the execution by a mob of an African American

5. ______________________ Black activist who favored taking action to obtain civil rights for blacks

6. ______________________ Wisconsin Senator who was a leading Progressive spokesman

7. ______________________ What country in addition to Cuba did the U.S. invade during the Spanish-American War?

8. ______________________ Elected President in 1896 and 1900

9. ______________________ Maximum length of workday proposed by Progressives

10. ______________________ Tactic used to prevent blacks from voting, it based the ability to vote in 1898 on who could vote in 1867

11. ______________________ Practice that justified racial segregation, upheld by *Plessy v. Ferguson* decision

12. ______________________ Politician who furthered the Progressive cause most on the national level

13. ______________________ Journalists and authors who exposed the abuses and failings in American life

14. ______________________ Tax paid to be able to vote; was a tactic to prevent blacks from voting

15. ______________________ Extreme Chinese nationalists who wanted to drive the "foreign devils" out of China in 1900

Quiz on Unit 19

Review the Student Review questions on Lessons 91-94

_____ 1. The 1900 U.S. population was about:
(a) 5 million
(b) 48 million
(c) 76 million
(d) 318 million

_____ 2. The percentage of the population that was considered rural in 1900 was:
(a) 20%
(b) 40%
(c) 60%
(d) 80%

_____ 3. The average life expectancy in the U.S. in 1900 was about:
(a) 28 years
(b) 47 years
(c) 55 years
(d) 78 years

_____ 4. What was the U.S. rank among countries of the world for industrial output in 1900?
(a) first
(b) second
(c) third
(d) fourth

_____ 5. John Dewey was influential in what field?
(a) library science
(b) steel
(c) politics
(d) education

_____ 6. The Chautauqua Movement:
(a) led the efforts at prohibition
(b) was the successor to the Progressive Movement
(c) brought speakers and entertainment to many towns and cities
(d) was begun by John Dewey

_____ 7. Theodore Roosevelt won the Nobel Prize for helping to bring an end to the:
(a) Russo-Japanese War
(b) Spanish-American War
(c) Crimean War
(d) Philippine War

_____ 8. Roosevelt's practice of filing suits to break up business trusts is called:
(a) price gouging
(b) trust-busting
(c) logrolling
(d) penny pinching

_____ 9. The situation in what country was the first test of the Roosevelt Corollary?
(a) Dominican Republic
(b) Cuba
(c) Chile
(d) Mexico

_____ 10. Who is credited with significant advances in mass production techniques?
(a) Theodore Roosevelt
(b) Alexander Graham Bell
(c) Gifford Pinchot
(d) Henry Ford

quiz continued on the next page

_____ 11. The first means of transit built across the isthmus of Panama was:

(a) an asphalt highway
(b) a railroad
(c) a sea-level canal
(d) a subway

_____ 12. Ferdinand de Lesseps:

(a) discovered the isthmus of Panama
(b) led the American construction of the Panama Canal
(c) led the revolution that created the Republic of Panama
(d) was involved in canal projects in both Suez and Panama

_____ 13. The French effort to build a canal across Panama failed because:

(a) the plan devised was not workable
(b) the technology and machinery needed did not exist
(c) the workforce was decimated by disease and accidents
(d) all of the above

_____ 14. The President most closely associated with the Panama Canal project was:

(a) William McKinley
(b) Theodore Roosevelt
(c) William Howard Taft
(d) Woodrow Wilson

_____ 15. For what invention is Guglielmo Marconi recognized?

(a) the chocolate bar
(b) the radio
(c) the steam shovel
(d) the telephone

Quiz on Unit 20

Review the Student Review questions on Lessons 96-99.

Matching

_____ 1. Federal Reserve System	A. Wilson's plan for settling war issues
_____ 2. Theodore Roosevelt	B. His assassination led to the Great War
_____ 3. Zimmerman Telegram	C. Formed to oversee companies involved in interstate commerce
_____ 4. Mexico	D. Rejected by the Senate
_____ 5. John J. Pershing	E. Republican nominee for President in 1916
_____ 6. Fourteen Points	F. Governor of New Jersey before becoming President
_____ 7. Charles Evans Hughes	G. Long-running military aspect of the Great War
_____ 8. Archduke Francis Ferdinand	H. German practice that challenged U.S. neutrality
_____ 9. League of Nations	I. Secretary of State for most of Wilson's first term
_____ 10. Treaty of Versailles	J. Enabled by the 16th Amendment, enacted by Congress
_____ 11. Reparations	K. British passenger liner sunk on May 7, 1915
_____ 12. Neutrality	L. Greatest individual hero of the Great War
_____ 13. Submarine warfare	M. American position when the Great War began
_____ 14. Trench warfare	N. 1912 Progressive Party presidential nominee
_____ 15. Personal income tax	O. Wilson's main objective at Versailles
_____ 16. Woodrow Wilson	P. Leader of the first American forces in Europe
_____ 17. William Jennings Bryan	Q. German overture to Mexico to fight against the U.S.
_____ 18. *Lusitania*	R. What Germany had to pay to victorious nations
_____ 19. Federal Trade Commission	S. Banking system begun in 1913
_____ 20. Alvin York	T. Dominated foreign policy in Wilson's first term

History Exam on Units 16-20

Review the quizzes on Units 16-20.

1. The main purpose of the Interstate Commerce Act was to regulate what industry? 1. ______________________

2. What is the term for the policy of using gold and silver as the standard for money? 2. ______________________

3. What was the third party formed in the early 1890s primarily by farmers who felt overlooked by the Republicans and Democrats? 3. ______________________

4. Who was the President assassinated in 1881 and succeeded by Chester Arthur? 4. ______________________

5. What term was used to describe southern Democrats after Reconstruction? 5. ______________________

6. Who was a pioneer in catalog sales? 6. ______________________

7. Who was the wealthiest leader in the oil industry? 7. ______________________

8. What is the name for a chartered business that is considered a legal person? 8. ______________________

9. Who was the black educator who founded Tuskegee Institute and accepted social segregation and discrimination? 9. ______________________

10. What Wisconsin Senator was a leading spokesman for Progressivism? 10. ______________________

11. What was the 1896 Supreme Court decision that upheld the practice of separate but equal facilities for blacks and whites? 11. ______________________

exam continued on the next page

12. What is the term used for journalists and authors who exposed the abuses and failings of American life? 12. ____________________

13. John Dewey was influential in what field? 13. ____________________

14. What was the movement that brought speakers and entertainment to many towns and cities? 14. ____________________

15. What term was given to the practice of Theodore Roosevelt's Administration of filing suits to break up business trusts? 15. ____________________

16. Who is the President most associated with encouraging the construction of the Panama Canal? 16. ____________________

17. What is the banking system begun in 1913? 17. ____________________

18. What was the British passenger liner sunk on May 7, 1915? 18. ____________________

19. What treaty that had been negotiated to end the Great War was defeated by the U.S. Senate? 19. ____________________

20. Who was the Secretary of State for most of Wilson's first term? 20. ____________________

English Exam on Units 16-20

This exam is based on the books In His Steps, Up from Slavery, *and* Mama's Bank Account. *Write a well-worded paragraph of about 75 words on each of the following subjects. You might want to review the literary analysis of these books in the Student Review.*

1. Based on your reading of *In His Steps,* what do you see as some of the costs and blessings of doing what you believe Jesus would do in every situation regardless of the consequences?

2. Based on your reading of *Up from Slavery,* what were some of the struggles that Booker T. Washington endured and overcame?

exam continued on the next page

3. Based on your reading of *Mama's Bank Account,* what are some of the benefits of having a parent you can respect and count on?

Bible Exam on Units 16-20

1. *During these units you read these hymns: "Let the Lower Lights Be Burning," "More Holiness Give Me," "Hallelujah! What a Savior!" "Blessed Assurance," "Tell Me the Story of Jesus," "A Wonderful Savior," and "O Master, Let Me Walk with Thee." Go back and re-read these hymns if necessary. Choose one and write a 100-word paragraph that tells why the message of the hymn is especially meaningful to you and how it helps your faith.*

exam continued on the next page

2. *In Lesson 85, we discussed how the social gospel movement attempted to put the message of Jesus into action to help people with their physical needs. However, more extreme proponents left behind teachings about personal salvation. Write a 100-word paragraph that expresses what you believe is the proper balance between helping others in their everyday lives and helping them become and grow as Christians. Cite Scripture in your paragraph.*

Quiz on Unit 21

Review the Student Review questions on Lessons 101-104.

_____ 1. The candidates for President and Vice President in 1920 were: for the Republicans, Warren Harding and Calvin Coolidge; for the Democrats, James Cox and who?
(a) William Jennings Bryan
(b) Franklin Roosevelt
(c) Al Smith
(d) Clarence Darrow

_____ 2. The Democratic candidate for President in 1928 was controversial because he was:
(a) from the South
(b) in legal trouble
(c) a Catholic
(d) a big businessman

_____ 3. The reparations and war debt payments that Germany had been required to pay were eventually:
(a) increased
(b) paid by the sale of land
(c) the only reason the Depression started
(d) cancelled

_____ 4. The McNairy-Haugen Bill proposed a farm pricing system based on:
(a) parity
(b) the value of gold
(c) the value of silver
(d) German reparations payments

_____ 5. The "noble experiment" was what Herbert Hoover called:
(a) immigration
(b) Prohibition
(c) radio
(d) automobiles

_____ 6. During the 1920s, immigration into the United States:
(a) was severely restricted
(b) about doubled over previous decades
(c) focused on people from China
(d) ceased

_____ 7. The number of radios and cars in use over the 1920s:
(a) increased dramatically
(b) stayed about the same
(c) dropped off significantly
(d) was never measured or estimated

_____ 8. The NAACP was founded in 1910 to:
(a) oversee college sports
(b) regulate the stock market
(c) help blacks
(d) enforce "separate but equal" laws

_____ 9. The rebirth of what group during the 1920s troubled blacks, Jews, Catholics, and other minorities?
(a) the Know-Nothing Party
(b) the Ku Klux Klan
(c) the Nativist League
(d) the America Only Party

_____ 10. The Kellogg-Briand Treaty was what?
(a) a pledge to eat more cereal
(b) a pledge to produce more cars
(c) a pledge to produce more food
(d) a pledge to abstain from war

Quiz on Unit 22

Review the Student Review questions on Lessons 106-109.

True or False

1. _____ President Hoover blamed the Depression on the Federal Reserve's monetary policy.

2. _____ At the worst point of the Depression, about one-fourth of the nation's workers were unemployed.

3. _____ Franklin Roosevelt was governor of New Jersey before being elected President.

4. _____ The overall name for FDR's program was the New Deal.

5. _____ The Civilian Conservation Corps cleared forest land and helped build state parks.

6. _____ Roosevelt took the United States monetary system off the gold standard.

7. _____ The TVA was a new experiment in unified planning for an entire region.

8. _____ Social Security provided unemployment and retirement benefits.

9. _____ Huey Long, the boss of Louisiana politics, was known as the Kingfish.

10. _____ The Dust Bowl was an area of Ohio and Indiana.

exam continued on the next page

11. _____ Many people who lived in the Dust Bowl moved to California.

12. _____ Humorist Will Rogers was a star of stage and screen in the early 1930s.

13. _____ Membership in conservative churches declined during the 1930s.

14. _____ Two popular forms of entertainment in the 1930s were television and the Internet.

15. _____ President Roosevelt withdrew diplomatic recognition of the U.S.S.R. in 1933.

16. _____ The Roosevelt Administration pursued a policy of being a partner and good neighbor with the countries of Latin America.

17. _____ The Reciprocal Trade Agreements Act created the status of most favored nation for countries conducting trade with the U.S.

18. _____ British Prime Minister Neville Chamberlain pursued a policy of military confrontations with Germany.

19. _____ Hitler, Mussolini, and Stalin were dictators who came to power before the Great War (World War I).

20. _____ World War II started on September 1, 1939 with Germany's invasion of Poland.

Quiz on Unit 23

Review the Student Review questions on Lessons 111-113 (only three lessons).

Matching, Part 1

_____ 1. Maginot Line	A. Allied invasion of northern France at Normandy
_____ 2. Dunkirk	B. Invaded by the Allies soon after victory in North Africa
_____ 3. Battle of Britain	C. Document of principles by Churchill and Roosevelt
_____ 4. Lend-Lease	D. U.S. offer to help nations resisting Axis aggression
_____ 5. Atlantic Charter	E. Attacked by Japanese on December 7, 1941
_____ 6. Pearl Harbor	F. German air attack on Britain, RAF defense
_____ 7. Philippines	G. MacArthur said "I shall return" when leaving here
_____ 8. Italy	H. First meeting of Churchill, Roosevelt, and Stalin
_____ 9. Tehran, Iran	I. French coastal city where the English evacuated troops
_____ 10. D-Day	J. Line of French defensive forts along border with Germany

Matching, Part 2

_____ 11. Manhattan Project	K. May 8, 1945, end of the war in Europe
_____ 12. Hiroshima	L. Where Japanese-Americans were interned during the war
_____ 13. Iwo Jima	M. German breakthrough in Belgium, December 1944
_____ 14. Yalta	N. Largest naval battle of World War II
_____ 15. Battle of the Bulge	O. Island near Japan taken at cost of 7,000 American lives
_____ 16. Leyte Gulf	P. Horrors discovered when Allies invaded Germany
_____ 17. Concentration camps	Q. Naval battles that stopped Japanese advance in Pacific
_____ 18. Relocation camps	R. February 1945 meeting of Churchill, Roosevelt, and Stalin
_____ 19. V-E Day	S. American project to develop an atomic bomb
_____ 20. Coral Sea, Midway Is.	T. Target of first atomic bomb

Quiz on Unit 24

Review the Student Review questions on Lessons 116-119.

_____ 1. The most powerful body in the United Nations is the:
(a) General Assembly
(b) Security Council
(c) Secretariat
(d) World Health Organization

_____ 2. The mutual defense organization of the U.S. and European countries is called:
(a) AFL-CIO
(b) MDO
(c) SEATO
(d) NATO

_____ 3. The Marshall Plan:
(a) focused on strengthening the U.S. military
(b) offered assistance to Communist China
(c) helped European nations rebuild after World War II
(d) sought to eliminate Communists in the U.S. State Department

_____ 4. The Communist attempt to cut off supplies to West Berlin was defeated by:
(a) the Berlin Airlift
(b) the Berlin Wall
(c) the Truman Doctrine
(d) Point Four

_____ 5. After World War II, Communists sought to expand their power in:
(a) Eastern Europe
(b) Greece
(c) Turkey
(d) all of the above

_____ 6. The Korean War began when:
(a) China started bombing South Korea
(b) South Korea invaded North Korea
(c) North Korea invaded South Korea
(d) MacArthur invaded at Inchon

_____ 7. The conflict between Truman and MacArthur over policy in Korea was resolved when:
(a) the war ended
(b) MacArthur resigned
(c) Truman fired MacArthur
(d) Truman recalled MacArthur

_____ 8. The atmosphere that Joseph McCarthy's accusations and hearings created was one of:
(a) fear and suspicion
(b) trust and calmness
(c) militant demonstrations
(d) generosity and kindness

_____ 9. Alger Hiss was accused of being a Communist by:
(a) Dean Acheson
(b) Julius Rosenberg
(c) Joseph McCarthy
(d) Whittaker Chambers

_____ 10. The Hollywood Ten were:
(a) actors who quit making films and enlisted in the Army
(b) Hollywood notables who appeared before a Congressional committee
(c) people who organized a demonstration in support of Alger Hiss
(d) stars who entertained troops in Korea during the conflict there.

quiz continued on the next page

_____ 11. The GI Bill:
(a) encouraged draftees to re-enlist
(b) gave benefits to veterans
(c) was an attempt to limit Soviet influence in Turkey
(d) provided officers for the Korean War

_____ 12. The generation born in the years following World War II is called:
(a) Bobby Soxers
(b) Baby Boomers
(c) Generation W
(d) the Greatest Generation

_____ 13. The first black player in major league baseball was:
(a) Smoky Burgess
(b) Eddie Lancaster
(c) Walt Williams
(d) Jackie Robinson

_____ 14. Truman furthered civil rights for blacks by:
(a) ordering the desegregation of the military
(b) appointing the first black Chief Justice
(c) desegregating schools in the District of Columbia
(d) selecting a black running mate in 1948

_____ 15. During the 1948 campaign, Truman called the Republican-led Congress:
(a) his allies in progress
(b) the Do-Nothing Congress
(c) a bunch of Communists
(d) Democrats in sheep's clothing

Quiz on Unit 25

Review the Student Review questions on Lessons 121-124.

Matching

_____ 1. Nikita Khrushchev	A. Inter-continental ballistic missile
_____ 2. Ho Chi Minh	B. Democratic presidential nominee in 1952 and 1956
_____ 3. U-2 incident	C. Focus of 1957 and 1960 Federal civil rights laws
_____ 4. Adlai Stevenson	D. Upheld "separate but equal" practice
_____ 5. Interstate Highway system	E. Russian satellite launched October 4, 1957
_____ 6. Kefauver Committee	F. Attempted to break away from Soviet control
_____ 7. Fidel Castro	G. Candidate for GOP presidential nomination in 1952 but lost out to Eisenhower
_____ 8. Voting rights	H. Said separate was inherently unequal
_____ 9. Rosa Parks	I. Scene of 1956 conflict over the Suez Canal
_____ 10. *Plessy v. Ferguson* (1896)	J. Labor organizations that merged in 1955
_____ 11. Little Rock	K. Took over space program from the military
_____ 12. Robert Taft	L. Got increased Federal funding after *Sputnik*
_____ 13. Egypt	M. Dramatic school integration crisis in 1957
_____ 14. *Brown v. Board of Ed.* (1954)	N. Her actions began Montgomery Bus Boycott
_____ 15. *Sputnik*	O. Investigated organized crime
_____ 16. NASA	P. When U.S.S.R. shot down U.S. spy plane
_____ 17. AFL and CIO	Q. Became Communist leader of Cuba in 1959
_____ 18. Hungary, 1956	R. Leader of the Soviet Union after Stalin
_____ 19. Public education	S. Transportation project begun by Eisenhower
_____ 20. ICBM	T. Declared Communist government in North Vietnam in 1945

History Exam on Units 21-25

Review the quizzes on Units 21-25.

On this exam you will be asked to list all the Presidents in order from Washington through Eisenhower.

Fill in the blanks with the correct answers from the Answer Bank on the third page of this exam.

The 1920 presidential election saw (1) ______________________________ take a prominent place on the American scene as the Democratic vice presidential candidate. During the 1920s, new laws (2) ______________________ immigration into the country. The number of cars and radios in use dramatically (3) ________________. The rebirth of the (4) ____________________ troubled blacks, Jews, Catholics, and other minority groups. International affairs took a back seat to Americans' desire to get back to their lives. The Kellogg-Briand Treaty was a pledge by the signing nations to abstain from (5) __________ except in self-defense. Germany had a difficult time paying the (6) __________________________ required by the Treaty of Versailles, and these payments were eventually (7) ______________________.

The stock market crash in October of 1929 started the Great Depression. At the worst point of the Depression, about (8) ___________________ of American workers were unemployed. Franklin Roosevelt, governor of (9) __________________, was elected President in 1932. He called his program for relief, recovery, and reform the (10) _________________. Congress created many new Federal agencies during this time. The (11) ____ cleared forest land and helped build state parks. The (12) __________ was a new experiment in unified planning for an entire region. (13) ______________________________ provided unemployment and retirement benefits. Adding to the misery of the times was the drought in the (14) _______________________, a large area in the Plains states. Roosevelt also took the U.S. monetary system off the (15) ______________________________ and gave diplomatic recognition to the (16) _________________. Meanwhile, events in other parts of the world increased concerns about the possibility of another war. (17) ____________, ____________, and Mussolini were dictators who came to power after the Great War (World War I). World War II started on September 1, 1939 when Germany invaded (18) _________________.

exam continued on the next page

The Allies struggled in the early days of the war. The British had to evacuate thousands of troops at the French city of (19) _______________. The Japanese attacked the United States at (20) ______________________________ on December 7, 1941. Germany launched a heavy air attack on the island of Great Britain, but the Royal Air Force fought back bravely and the British people never gave up. Winston Churchill called this conflict the (21) ______________________________________. General Douglas MacArthur had to withdraw from (22) ________________________________ in 1942, but he vowed, "I shall return." But the Allies fought back bravely. The naval battles at (23) ______________________________________ halted the Japanese advance in the Pacific. The massive Allied invasion of France on June 6, 1944, commonly called (24) _____________, began the fall of Germany. May 8, 1945 was celebrated as (25) _________________, the end of the war in Europe. The end of the war with Japan came soon after the U.S. dropped atomic bombs on (26) ____________________ and Nagasaki.

The United Nations began in 1945. The most powerful body in that organization is the (27) ________________________________. The (28) ________________________________ helped European nations rebuild. A new reality confronted the world after the war. A new enemy to world peace appeared in the form of Communism and the Soviet Union. The Communist attempt to cut off supplies to West Berlin was defeated by the (29) _________________________. Communist (30) ______________________ invaded South Korea to begin the Korean War. Senator Joseph McCarthy capitalized on a concern about Communist infiltration in the United States to create an atmosphere of (31) ____. However, Whittaker Chambers revealed the presence of one Communist in the Federal government when he accused (32) __________________________ of being a Communist. The accused man later went to prison for perjury when he denied being a Communist. The late 1940s saw an increased concern for equal rights for blacks. President Harry Truman ordered that the (33) ___________________ be desegregated. (34) _________________________________ broke the color line in baseball by becoming the first African American in the major leagues.

Many changes and challenges faced the U.S. in the 1950s. Dwight Eisenhower was elected president in 1952 and 1956, both times defeating (35) ___________________________________. Eisenhower encouraged the major transportation project of the (36) _______________ ________________________________. The Russian launch of the (37) ________________

exam continued on the next page

satellite punctured American pride and caused the country to place a greater emphasis on science and space exploration. Meanwhile, the ferment for greater civil rights for blacks continued to build. The U.S. Supreme Court ruled in 1954 that maintaining so-called (38) ________________________ school facilities for blacks and whites was unconstitutional. Rosa Parks' refusal to give up her seat on a bus to a white man led to the (39) ________________________. A dramatic school integration crisis took place in (40) ________________ in 1957.

Answer Bank

Sputnik	Hitler, Stalin
Montgomery Bus Boycott	separate but equal
Security Council	Civilian Conservation Corps (CCC)
Adlai Stevenson	Hiroshima
V-E Day	Interstate Highway system
TVA	New Deal
fear and suspicion	Coral Sea and Midway Island
war	increased
Jackie Robinson	North Korea
the Philippines	gold standard
Little Rock	Marshall Plan
Social Security	U.S.S.R.
Battle of Britain	restricted
Alger Hiss	Poland
Pearl Harbor	one fourth
Franklin Roosevelt	reparations
military	Berlin Airlift
Dunkirk	D-Day
cancelled	New York
Dust Bowl	Ku Klux Klan

exam continued on the next page

41-57. Complete this list of the first thirty-four presidents in order.

1. ______________________________
2. John Adams
3. ______________________________
4. James Madison
5. ______________________________
6. John Quincy Adams
7. ______________________________
8. Martin Van Buren
9. ______________________________
10. John Tyler
11. ______________________________
12. Zachary Taylor
13. ______________________________
14. Franklin Pierce
15. ______________________________
16. Abraham Lincoln
17. ______________________________
18. Ulysses S. Grant
19. ______________________________
20. James Garfield
21. ______________________________
22. Grover Cleveland
23. ______________________________
24. Grover Cleveland
25. ______________________________
26. Theodore Roosevelt
27. ______________________________
28. Woodrow Wilson
29. ______________________________
30. Calvin Coolidge
31. ______________________________
32. Franklin D. Roosevelt
33. ______________________________
34. Dwight D. Eisenhower

English Exam for Units 21-25

As you continue your education, one thing you will probably have to do is compare and contrast works of literature, sometimes ones that don't seem very similar. You will need to think about how they are similar and in what ways they are different.

On a separate piece of paper, write a 300-word essay with five paragraphs comparing and contrasting *Miracle in the Hills* and *To Kill a Mockingbird*. Begin by noting that both books are set in the rural South in the first part of the twentieth century. Discuss the similarities and differences in the way the books deal with these issues:

- community expectations
- prejudice and learning new ways
- who brought change and how
- what part children play in each story
- what you learned by reading each book

Bible Exam for Units 21-25

This exam covers Lessons 105, 110, 115, 120, and 125. Write a paragraph on each of the following topics.

1. What do you think has been the impact of the Scopes trial on American thought, American Christianity, and the creation versus evolution debate? (Lesson 105)

2. Summarize your understanding of the issue of suffering and the encouragement you get from Scripture related to it. (Lesson 110)

3. How do you see the spiritual war that is going on in our country? What are the battlefields, the weapons, and the best strategy for victory in your life and in your family? (Lesson 115)

exam continued on the next page

4. To what degree do you think the Christian religion should be recognized and encouraged in the American public square (for instance, in public schools, parks, government buildings, and by governmental bodies)? (Lesson 120)

5. How has the practice and influence of Christianity changed in the U.S. since the 1950s? (Lesson 125)

Quiz on Unit 26

Review the Student Review questions on Lessons 126-129.

Matching

_____ 1. Major party presidential candidates in 1960	A. Martin Luther King Jr.
_____ 2. Kennedy's legislative program	B. Tet
_____ 3. Failed attempt to invade Cuba by anti-Castro forces	C. Sit-ins
_____ 4. Lyndon Johnson's legislative program	D. New Frontier
_____ 5. Republican presidential candidate in 1964	E. Gulf of Tonkin Resolution
_____ 6. Affected by Supreme Court decisions in the 1960s	F. Robert F. Kennedy
_____ 7. Tactic by blacks to integrate lunch counters	G. Lyndon B. Johnson
_____ 8. Communist guerrillas in South Vietnam	H. Kennedy and Nixon
_____ 9. Permitted U.S. build-up in Vietnam	I. Barry Goldwater
_____ 10. Civil rights leader assassinated in 1968	J. Hubert Humphrey
_____ 11. Presidential candidate assassinated in 1968	K. Rights of accused persons
_____ 12. Communist offensive that hurt U.S. cause	L. George Wallace
_____ 13. Decided not to run for President in 1968	M. Great Society
_____ 14. Democratic presidential candidate in 1968	N. Viet Cong
_____ 15. Independent presidential candidate in 1968	O. Bay of Pigs

Quiz on Unit 27

Review the Student Review questions on Lessons 131-134.

_____ 1. A deadly clash between college students and National Guardsmen took place at:
(a) Harvard University
(b) Arizona State University
(c) Kent State University
(d) Idaho State University

_____ 2. Part of President Nixon's plan to end the Vietnam War was:
(a) invading North Vietnam with U.S. troops
(b) using low-power nuclear weapons
(c) asking the Soviet Union to help defeat North Vietnam
(d) bombing Communist sites in Cambodia

_____ 3. The Pentagon Papers were:
(a) orders sent by President Nixon to the Pentagon
(b) policy statements issued by the military regarding Vietnam
(c) underground newspapers printed in the Pentagon critical of military actions
(d) secret Pentagon documents leaked to the press by Daniel Ellsberg

_____ 4. After the U.S. pulled out of Vietnam:
(a) North and South Vietnam signed a peace treaty
(b) other nations came to the aid of South Vietnam
(c) the South Vietnamese government and military collapsed
(d) the U.S. took over Cambodia

_____ 5. A disruption in the availability of gasoline in the U.S. was caused by:
(a) oil tankers being sunk in the Atlantic
(b) a strike by oil workers in the U.S.
(c) the decision by OPEC to cut oil sales
(d) debates over development of solar power

_____ 6. Man first landed on the moon in what year?
(a) 1963
(b) 1965
(c) 1967
(d) 1969

_____ 7. President Nixon made bold foreign policy moves by visiting:
(a) Communist China and the Soviet Union
(b) North Vietnam and Cuba
(c) Egypt and Jordan
(d) Israel and Egypt

_____ 8. The Democratic presidential nominee in 1972 was:
(a) George Wallace
(b) George McGovern
(c) Nelson Rockefeller
(d) Edward Kennedy

_____ 9. Nixon's failure in the Watergate scandal was that:
(a) he participated in the cover-up of the scandal and obstructed the investigation of it
(b) he lied under oath before the House Judiciary Committee
(c) he used information obtained illegally from the Democratic Party headquarters
(d) he did not ask Senate Republicans to support him

quiz continued on the next page

_____ 10. How far did impeachment proceedings against Nixon develop?
(a) A resolution calling for impeachment was introduced in the House.
(b) The House Judiciary Committee approved articles of impeachment.
(c) The full House voted in favor of impeachment.
(d) The Senate began an impeachment trial.

_____ 11. Gerald Ford:
(a) won the presidential election of 1974
(b) was minority leader of the House before becoming Vice President
(c) resigned one month after taking office
(d) never was Vice President

_____ 12. A serious economic problem during Carter's presidency was:
(a) a dramatic increase in taxes
(b) salary schedules for Federal workers
(c) the high rate of inflation
(d) the number of union strikes

_____ 13. President Carter oversaw talks at Camp David that led to an agreement between:
(a) Egypt and Iraq
(b) Israel and the Soviet Union
(c) China and Vietnam
(d) Egypt and Israel

_____ 14. Many Americans became more aware of Islam because:
(a) a Muslim ran for President on a third party ticket in 1972
(b) trade with Muslim nations increased after oil was discovered there in 1975
(c) two Muslims were elected to Congress in 1976
(d) fundamentalist Muslims took Americans hostage in Iran in 1979

_____ 15. Jimmy Carter implemented a policy of:
(a) limiting foreign aid to countries with poor human rights records
(b) free trade with Canada
(c) increased foreign aid to countries in the Balkan Peninsula
(d) meeting with South American leaders once per month

Quiz on Unit 28

Review the Student Review questions on Lessons 136-139.

Matching

_____ 1. Walter Mondale	A. Served as governor of California
_____ 2. Jerry Falwell	B. Founded the Moral Majority
_____ 3. Colin Powell	C. Congressman, UN ambassador, Vice President, President
_____ 4. Jimmy Carter	D. Appointed to serve on the U.S. Supreme Court
_____ 5. George H. W. Bush	E. Defeated by Ronald Reagan in 1980
_____ 6. Ronald Reagan	F. Chairman of the Joint Chiefs of Staff
_____ 7. Clarence Thomas	G. Defeated by Ronald Reagan in 1984

Multiple Choice

_____ 8. What was the name given to America's reusable space craft?
(a) Space Shuttle
(b) Space Taxi
(c) Multi-Use Space Station
(d) Apollo Space Vehicle

_____ 9. What did President Reagan once call the Soviet Union?
(a) our brothers in progress
(b) more democratic than Communist
(c) an evil empire
(d) the beast of Revelation

_____ 10. What did Reagan challenge Soviet leader Gorbachev to do?
(a) stop giving aid to Communist China
(b) give voting rights to women
(c) meet with the pope in Rome
(d) tear down the Berlin Wall

_____ 11. The Iran-Contra scandal involved:
(a) a secret arms deal with Iran
(b) an attempt to help free American hostages
(c) undercover assistance to Central American freedom fighters
(d) all of the above

quiz continued on the next page

_____ 12. The industry that collapsed during the George H. W. Bush presidency was:
(a) the vinyl record industry
(b) the corded phone industry
(c) the savings and loan industry
(d) the American toy industry

_____ 13. The independent labor union in Communist Poland that sought recognition was:
(a) Defiance
(b) Solidarity
(c) Poland Forever
(d) Independence

_____ 14. What event in November 1989 symbolized the fall of Communism?
(a) The Berlin Wall was torn down.
(b) Vietnam allowed free elections.
(c) Poland made the Roman Catholic Church its official state religion.
(d) Gorbachev met with the Dalai Lama.

_____ 15. The allied military operation that pushed Iraqi forces out of Kuwait was called:
(a) Operation Desert Oasis
(b) Operation Desert Storm
(c) Operation Kick 'Em from Kuwait
(d) Operation Slam Saddam

Quiz on Unit 29

Review the Student Review questions on Lessons 141-144.

Matching, Part 1

_____ 1. Slobodan Milosevic	A. Waco cult that had a standoff with Federal officials
_____ 2. Bob Dole	B. Prime minister of Israel assassinated in 1995
_____ 3. DJIA	C. Vice President under Bill Clinton
_____ 4. Jeff Bezos	D. 1992 and 1996 Reform Party candidate for President
_____ 5. Branch Davidians	E. Leader of Yugoslavia charged with war crimes
_____ 6. 1944	F. Republicans gained control of U.S. House and Senate
_____ 7. Ross Perot	G. Governor of Arkansas before becoming President
_____ 8. Impeachment trial	H. The issue that hurt George H. W. Bush most in 1992
_____ 9. Bill Clinton	I. Republican Senator and 1996 presidential candidate
_____ 10. Yitzak Rabin	J. Founder of Amazon.com
_____ 11. The economy	K. Dow Jones Industrial Average
_____ 12. Al Gore	L. Federal Reserve Board, guides U.S. monetary policy
_____ 13. 1994	M. Failed attempt to remove Clinton from office
_____ 14. The Fed	N. First electronic computer built

Matching, Part 2

_____ 15. Contract with America	O. U.S. helped its president, Jean-Bertrand Aristide
_____ 16. NAFTA	P. 1994 Republican election promise
_____ 17. Whitewater	Q. Province of Yugoslavia that wanted independence
_____ 18. Haiti	R. Force that took action against Yugoslavia in 1998
_____ 19. Kosovo	S. Trade deal involving Mexico, Canada, and the U.S.
_____ 20. NATO	T. Project for which the Clintons were investigated

Quiz on Unit 30

Review the Student Review questions on Lessons 146-149.

True or False

_____ 1. In 2010, the official population of the United States was over 308 million.

_____ 2. The most populous state in 2000 was New York.

_____ 3. The most populous urban metropolitan area in 2000 was New York City.

_____ 4. The U.S. had a total of about 50 million households in 2000.

_____ 5. The U.S. gross domestic product in 2000 was about six billion dollars.

_____ 6. The largest single religious group in the U.S. in 2000 was the Roman Catholic Church.

_____ 7. In the 2000 presidential election, George W. Bush won the popular vote.

_____ 8. Controversy over the election returns in 2000 centered in Florida.

_____ 9. The final decision on the 2000 presidential election was made in practical terms by the U.S. Supreme Court.

_____ 10. The September 11, 2001 terrorist attacks involved the hijacking of six passenger planes.

_____ 11. One of the hijacked planes on September 11, 21001, hit the U.S. Capitol building.

_____ 12. The mastermind of the September 11 attacks was Osama bin Laden.

_____ 13. After the September 11 attacks, U.S. and other coalition forces attacked Afghanistan and Iraq.

_____ 14. Osama bin Laden was discovered and killed by Navy SEAL forces in Saudi Arabia.

_____ 15. The Democratic presidential candidate in 2004 was Al Gore.

_____ 16. The credit crunch that climaxed in the fall of 2008 was the result at least in part of large-scale failures in home mortgages.

exam continued on the next page

_____ 17. Another common term for a less than excellent credit history is underwater.

_____ 18. When Barack Obama was nominated for President in 2008, he was Governor of Illinois.

_____ 19. The comprehensive legislation passed in 2010 that Obama had pledged to work toward was the Patient Protection and Affordable Care Act, often called "Obamacare."

_____ 20. In December of 2009 Barack Obama was awarded the Nobel Peace Prize.

History Exam on Units 26-30

Review the quizzes on Units 26-30.

On this exam you will be asked to complete a list of all the Presidents in order from Washington through Trump.

Fill in the blanks with the correct answers from the Answer Bank.

In the 1960 presidential contest, (1) ______________________________ defeated Richard Nixon. The new president called his legislative program the (2) ______________________________. His administration was embarrassed by the failed attempt to invade Cuba with anti-Castro forces at the (3) ______________________________. After the tragic assassination of this Chief Executive, Lyndon Johnson became President. Johnson called his program the (4) ____________________ ____________________. During Johnson's time in office, the American involvement in Vietnam grew. The (5) ____ was the justification for sending more troops and materiel to Vietnam. Civil rights leader (6) ____________________ ____________________ was assassinated in 1968, as was Democratic senator and presidential candidate (7) ______________________________. Johnson decided not to run again in 1968, and the Democratic nomination went to his Vice President, (8) ____________________ ______________________. Nixon was the Republican nominee, but the race was complicated by the independent candidacy of (9) __________________________________.

After Nixon won, he pursued his strategy of ending the war in Vietnam, which included the tactic of (10) ____. Several years later, the U.S. pulled out of Vietnam, and the result was that (11)____. South Vietnam fell to the Communists, and North and South Vietnam became unified under Communist rule. America faced an energy crisis in the early 1970s because of (12) ____. President Nixon made bold foreign policy moves when he visited (13) ____________________ ____________________________________ in 1972.

exam continued on the next page

Also during Nixon's presidency, the nation achieved an important space milestone in 1969 when the (14) ____.

However, the Nixon Administration was engulfed by the Watergate scandal. Nixon's involvement included (15) ____

____.

After the House Judiciary Committee (16) ______________________________

______________________________, Nixon resigned and Gerald Ford became President. During Jimmy Carter's term, the economy suffered with a (17) ______________

______________________________ and high interest rates. However, Carter was able to bring about an agreement between (18) ______________________________ at the Camp David summit talks.

In 1980 Ronald Reagan was elected President. He had earlier served as governor of (19) ____________________. Reagan took a hard line against Communism. He once called the Soviet Union an (20) ____________________. He challenged Soviet leader Mikhail Gorbachev to (21) ______________________________. Reagan had his own problems because of the (22) ______________________________, which involved a secret arms deal, an attempt to negotiate the release of American hostages, and undercover assistance to Central American freedom fighters. After George H. W. Bush became President, the nation struggled through the collapse of the (23) ________________________ industry. The collapse of Communism in Europe was epitomized in 1989 when the (24) ______________________________________. Near the end of Bush's term, Iraq invaded neighboring Kuwait. The multi-national effort to push the Iraqi forces out of Kuwait was called (25) ______________________________________.

Bill Clinton, governor of (26) ____________________, was elected president in 1992 and 1996. The Democrats' rise in power was disrupted in 1994, however, when the Republicans (27) ____.

Clinton had to face an (28) ______________________________________ during his second term, but the effort to remove him from office failed. Clinton succeeded in seeing NAFTA, a (29) ____, go into effect.

exam continued on the next page

The 2000 presidential election was marked by controversy over the returns in the state of (30) ____________________. The issue was finally decided by the U.S. Supreme Court. The nation endured the terrorist attacks of (31) ______________________________. The attacks were masterminded by (32) ____________________________, who was later killed by Navy SEAL forces during the presidency of Barack Obama. Near the end of George W. Bush's presidency, the nation suffered a credit crunch and recession caused in part by large-scale failures in (33) ____________________________.

Answer Bank

Arkansas	Osama bin Laden
George Wallace	evil empire
Gulf of Tonkin Resolution	John Kennedy
California	trade deal involving the U.S., Canada, and Mexico
China and the Soviet Union	gained conitrol of the U.S. House and Senate
Bay of Pigs	New Frontier
Hubert Humphrey	Robert Kennedy
approved articles of impeachment	Iran-Contra scandal
Operation Desert Storm	Martin Luther King Jr.
tear down the Berlin Wall	bombing Communist sites in Cambodia
September 11, 2001	high rate of inflation
Great Society	Berlin Wall was torn down
home mortgages	participating in the cover-up of the scandal and obstructing the investigation of it
Florida	first men landed on the moon
savings and loan	the decision by OPEC to cut oil sales
impeachment trial	the South Vietnamese government and military collapsed
Israel and Egypt	

exam continued on the next page

Complete this list of the presidents of the United States in order from memory.

1. George Washington
2. ____________________
3. Thomas Jefferson
4. ____________________
5. James Monroe
6. ____________________
7. Andrew Jackson
8. ____________________
9. William Henry Harrison
10. ____________________
11. James K. Polk
12. ____________________
13. Millard Fillmore
14. ____________________
15. James Buchanan
16. ____________________
17. Andrew Johnson
18. ____________________
19. Rutherford B. Hayes
20. ____________________
21. Chester A. Arthur
22. ____________________
23. Benjamin Harrison
24. ____________________
25. William McKinley
26. ____________________
27. William Howard Taft
28. ____________________
29. Warren G. Harding
30. ____________________
31. Herbert Hoover
32. ____________________
33. Harry Truman
34. ____________________
35. John F. Kennedy
36. ____________________
37. Richard Nixon
38. ____________________
39. Jimmy Carter
40. ____________________
41. George H. W. Bush
42. ____________________
43. George W. Bush
44. ____________________
45. Donald Trump

English Exam on Units 26-30

This exam covers The Giver, *one poem in* American Voices, *and your general reaction to material by and about African Americans.*

_____ 1. What is the event at which Jonas receives his assignment?
(a) Day of Rejoicing
(b) Procedure of Assignment
(c) Ceremony of Twelve
(d) Coming Out

_____ 2. What word does the Giver use to describe life with no changes and no color?
(a) routine
(b) sameness
(c) monotony
(d) monochromal

3. Discuss the meaning of this statement: "When we have a past, we have a future."

____

____

____

____

4. What is one lesson that you learned by reading *The Giver*?

____

____

____

____

5. What event is commemorated by the poem, "A Day in July" (*American Voices*, page 355)?

____

6. During this course you have read *Narrative of the Life of Frederick Douglass, Uncle Tom's Cabin, Up from Slavery,* and *To Kill a Mockingbird*. You have read poems by Phillis Wheatley, Frances E. W. Harper, and Paul Laurence Dunbar. You have read essays or speeches by Frederick Douglass, W. E. B. Du Bois, Booker T. Washington, Martin Luther King Jr., and Clarence Thomas. You have read portions of the *Brown v. Board of Education* Supreme Court decision. Give some thought to the experience of African Americans in this country and write on a separate sheet of paper an essay of 200-250 words expressing your thoughts. You might include: being taken from their homeland; enduring slavery; gaining freedom but enduring discrimination and segregation; working for equality; and seeing many African Americans achieve success in many fields, including being elected President of the United States.

Bible Exam on Units 26-30

Review the Lesson Review questions on Lessons 130, 135, 140, 145, and 150.

_____ 1. When Jesus talked about the religious establishment of His day:
(a) He said only positive things.
(b) He said the leaders were hypocrites.
(c) He complimented their clothing
(d) He encouraged them to make a new translation of the Scriptures.

_____ 2. The followers of Jesus:
(a) have often helped change the world
(b) have all withdrawn from the world
(c) have all become like the world
(d) have all moved away from where they grew up to different parts of the world

_____ 3. The Bible calls the unborn John the Baptist:
(a) a blob of tissue
(b) an inconvenience
(c) a potential human being
(d) a baby

_____ 4. Before the Roe v. Wade Supreme Court decision:
(a) restrictions on abortions were common
(b) no state regulated abortions
(c) the Court had said that a fetus is a person
(d) women could not obtain abortions in the U.S.

_____ 5. The letter to the Philippians is a lesson on:
(a) the details of Christ's second coming
(b) how to get a local church to be active
(c) the obligation of Christians in Philippi to recognize Paul's apostleship
(d) having a positive attitude, especially in difficult circumstances

_____ 6. In Philippians,what principle did Paul say guided his life?
(a) Live and let live.
(b) It doesn't matter what you do as long as you are happy.
(c) To live is Christ, to die is gain.
(d) A penny saved is a penny earned.

_____ 7. What is a person's first responsibility?
(a) to maintain a balanced budget
(b) to vote the right way
(c) to make sure his or her life is right before God
(d) to enjoy American history in high school

exam continued on the next page

_____ 8. What is one thing all human beings have in common?
(a) We all have the same abilities.
(b) We are imperfect.
(c) We are all ashamed of our wrong actions.
(d) We all have the same intelligence.

_____ 9. What has been a major factor in America since the founding of English colonies?
(a) the Christian religion
(b) the national banking system
(c) fair treatment of people of color
(d) the electoral college

_____ 10. What is more important than being admired for what we have?
(a) having a catchy national anthem
(b) being admired for who we are
(c) having the latest technology
(d) having the highest industrial output in the world

11. What are your thoughts on the significance of the private lives of public leaders?

____

____

____

____

____

____

____

____

12. What has been the impact of studying *Exploring America* on your faith and your view of the United States?

____

____

____

____

____

____

____

____